INSIDE MAGIC

ALAKAZAM!
SENSATIONAL MAGIC TRICKS WITH SILK, THIMBLES, PAPER, AND MONEY

Nicholas Einhorn

rosen publishing's
rosen
central

New York

This edition published in 2013 by:

The Rosen Publishing Group, Inc.
29 East 21st Street
New York, NY 10010

Library of Congress Cataloging-in-Publication Date

Einhorn, Nicholas
Alakazam!: sensational magic tricks with silk, thimbles, paper, and money/Nicholas Einhorn.
    p. cm. – (Inside magic)
Includes bibliographical references and index.
Summary: This book presents instructions for forty-two magic tricks including producing silk from mid-air, making a thimble disappear, making money appear, and many more.
ISBN 978-1-4488-9221-1 (library binding)
1. Magic tricks—Juvenile literature [1. Magic tricks] I. Title II. Series 2013
793.8—dc23

Manufactured in the United States of America

CPSIA Compliance Information: Batch #W13YA: For farther information, contact Rosen Publishing, New York, New York, at 1-800-237-9932.

Copyright in design, text and images © Anness Publishing Limited, U.K. 2002, 2013. Originally published as part of a larger volume: *The Art of Magic.*

CONTENTS

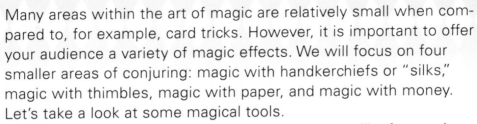

INTRODUCTION

Many areas within the art of magic are relatively small when compared to, for example, card tricks. However, it is important to offer your audience a variety of magic effects. We will focus on four smaller areas of conjuring: magic with handkerchiefs or "silks," magic with thimbles, magic with paper, and magic with money. Let's take a look at some magical tools.

Magicians call handkerchiefs "silks." The best silks for magic are the ones found in magic shops, but any thin, silk handkerchief will do. Silks can be used for any number of tricks contained in this book, and they come in a variety of sizes and colors.

Paper can usually be found at home. But for special colors, check out party and paper goods stores.

You may have a thimble lying around your house. (If not, thimbles can be found at a fabric or craft store.) One of the earliest known references to thimble magic is in *The Art of Modern Conjuring* by Professor Henry Garenne, published in 1879. The trick was entitled "The Travelling Thimble." Since then, magicians have invented many ways to make thimbles multiply, change color, penetrate handkerchiefs, appear, and disappear. Magicians who perform traditional stage acts often feature thimbles as part of their program.

Money is the one thing that most people carry with them at all times. Probably the most popular trick using money is to make it appear out of thin air. The idea of producing money out of thin air was born a long time ago. There cannot be many children who have never had a coin pulled from behind their ear. For general coin tricks, you can use any coins, but most magicians favor the half-dollar for its size, weight, and gripping qualities.

Remember, all magic tricks require dexterity and lots of practice! Ask any seasoned magician for tips, and he or she will definitely say that the most important thing to do when learning any magic trick is to practice. You can buy all the pieces of magic equipment you want, but without practice, you'll never be able to pull off any of your tricks. Try practicing in front of the mirror. And then try practicing in front of your friends and family. Ask your practice audience to keep an eye out for mistakes and then work to fix them. Once you've perfected some of your best tricks, you can try them out on a wider audience and maybe even set up some performances for the public!

silk magic

There are literally thousands of tricks you can do with handkerchiefs, and some of these are described here. You should not aim to put together a whole show of handkerchief magic, as this may be a little tiresome for your audience. However, handkerchief tricks can be very spectacular, and if you use them as part of your act you can make a big impression on your audience.

simple silk production

There are dozens of ways to produce a silk from thin air. This version and the Mid-Air Silk Production which follows are two of the easiest and most magical. For extra effect, sprinkle confetti or glitter into the folds as you prepare the silk.

1. To prepare, place a silk handkerchief in front of you, completely flat and with one corner toward you.

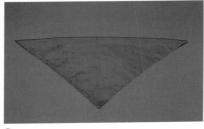

2. Fold the silk away from you, in half and along the diagonal.

3. Begin rolling the silk from the fold. Try to make the roll as tight and neat as possible.

4. Continue rolling the silk until you reach the far corner.

5. Roll the silk from one end to the other, again trying to ensure a tight, neat roll.

6. Leave a tiny "ear" of silk at the end, as shown here.

Secret View

7. Grip the rolled silk in the right-hand as shown so that the "ear" of the silk is clipped tightly between your right thumb and first finger.

8. Viewed from the front, if the hand is held naturally, the silk is completely hidden. With your right hand, point to an imaginary spot in the air to your left, at about chest level.

9. Reach up to that point and simultaneously, with a gentle jerk of the right hand, let the silk un-roll, ready for use in another trick.

mid-air silk production

The magician's hand is shown unmistakably empty but as they reach into the air a beautiful silk appears! Practice is required to make this always look good, but the result is so spectacular it is well worth the effort. It makes an ideal opening trick.

1. For this trick you must be wearing a jacket or long-sleeved shirt. To prepare, bunch up a silk handkerchief in your left hand. The bundle should be very small.

2. Extend your right arm and push the silk into the crook of your elbow, covering the silk with a fold of cloth from the sleeve.

3. Keeping the right elbow slightly bent will ensure the silk remains hidden. You are now ready to begin performing the trick.

4. Show that both hands are completely empty. Keep the arms bent just enough to prevent the silk from being exposed. (This restriction of movement is the reason why the Mid-Air Silk Production is a good trick to open with.)

5. This side view shows what happens next. The right hand quickly and sharply reaches up into the air, snapping open the fabric at the right elbow. The silk is catapulted up into the air and is caught by the right hand.

6. From the front, the silk seems to appear from nowhere!

rose to silk

A red rose worn on the magician's lapel is dramatically changed into silk. It would also be possible to add the prepared silk to a bunch of real roses. The magician could then pluck the top of a rose off a specially prepared stem as an alternative to his lapel.

1. You will need to wear a jacket with a buttonhole on the lapel. To prepare, lay a silk handkerchief flat, with one of the corners pointing toward you.

2. Begin rolling the silk toward the top corner. Try to make the roll as tight as possible. The neater you roll the silk, the better the rose will look.

3. Continue rolling until you reach the opposite corner.

4. At one end, bend the corner at right angles to create an "ear."

5. Starting at this end, tightly roll the silk to the opposite end. You will start to form a small bundle.

6. The finished bundle should resemble a rose. Leave a small amount of silk at the end of the roll.

7. With a match or similar object, tuck the loose end into the fold to hold the bundle in position.

8. Push the loose end all the way through to the back of the silk, being careful not to ruin the folds that make up the rose.

9. Take this loose end and push it through the buttonhole in your lapel. You are now ready to perform. At a glance, it will look just as though you are wearing a rose in your buttonhole.

10. With your left hand, hold the rose in place by gently squeezing the sides. With your right fingers, grip the center of the rose (the "ear").

11. Gently pull the "ear" outward, and the rose will visibly start to transform into a large silk.

12. Stretch the silk between both hands and wait for the applause! Try using some glitter or cutting up some tissue paper into small confetti-sized pieces and inserting them into the silk when you fold it. As the silk is pulled from the lapel, the contents will cascade to the floor, adding an extra magical effect.

pencil through silk

A silk handkerchief is draped over a pencil, which is pushed straight through the center of the silk. The handkerchief is displayed to show that it is completely unharmed. This kind of impromptu magic gives you the ability to perform a miracle with objects that can be borrowed.

1. Hold a corner of a silk handkerchief in your left hand and display a pencil in your right fingertips.

2. Drape the silk over the top of the pencil so that the center lies on the point of the pencil.

3. Close your left hand around the pencil so that the shape can clearly be seen through the fabric.

Secret View

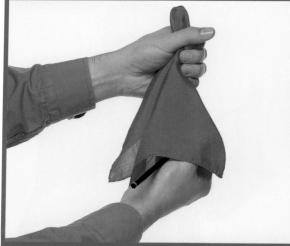

4. At the same moment, secretly bend your right hand at the wrist to bring the pencil back to a position outside the silk. From the front, this move is unseen and the silk continues to hold the shape of the pencil.

5. Immediately maneuver the pencil back up to a position behind the silk and under the left thumb. The moves in steps 3 and 4 are achieved in one swift motion, and should only take about one second.

Secret View

6. Give the pencil a push upward, and the tip will appear to penetrate the silk. In reality the pencil simply slides up against the silk and into view.

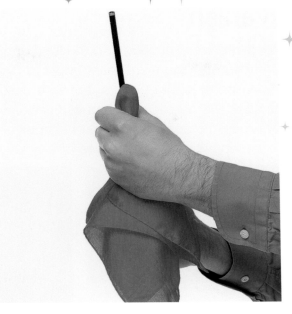

7. From the front, the illusion is perfect and your audience will believe the pencil has really been pushed through the middle of the silk handkerchief.

8. Pull the pencil completely free of the silk and once again display the pencil in your right fingertips.

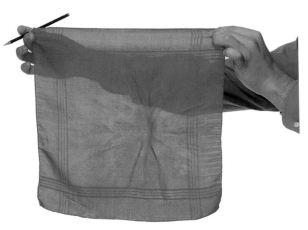

9. Open the silk between both hands to show that it is undamaged. You can hand both the silk and the pencil to your spectators for examination, and then perhaps use the same items for your next trick.

silk vanish

A silk handkerchief is pushed into the left hand. After a suitable flourish, the hand is shown completely empty! There are many ways to "vanish" a silk. This trick uses what magicians call a "pull"—a secret holder worn out of sight, usually under a jacket. The item to be vanished is placed inside. The holder is then pulled back into the jacket by a piece of elastic. Pulls are available from magic shops in a variety of shapes and sizes, but you can easily make your own. Pulls can also be worn within the sleeves of a jacket.

1. To make the "pull," remove the lid from a 35mm film canister and cut a hole about ¾in (2cm) in diameter. Pierce a small hole in the bottom of the canister and, with a simple knot inside, attach a piece of elastic approximately 24in (60cm) long. (The length depends on your waist size. For greater strength, cut double the length and fold the elastic in half.) Attach a safety pin to the free end of the elastic. Put the lid back on the canister.

2. Thread the elastic through your belt loops from your left side around to your right side. Attach the safety pin to a loop on the right of your body. It may take several attempts to find the correct position for the "pull" and the elastic may need to be cut down or adjusted.

3. The canister should rest at a position approximately in line with your pants pocket, and the tension of the elastic should hold it loosely but firmly against the belt loop. Test the operation of the "pull" by pulling the canister away from the belt loop to a position in front of your chest. Let the canister go, and it should return to the position it started in. If not, readjust the gimmick.

Secret View

4. In performance, hold the "pull" in your left hand. Stretch out the elastic so that your left hand can maintain a position just in front of your body. Be careful not to pull open your jacket and reveal your secret—this is an exposed view of the position you should be in.

5. Show the silk handkerchief in your right hand. Pretend to insert it into your left hand. In reality, you are pushing it into the canister through the hole in the lid.

6. Continue pushing the silk into your hand until it is completely contained within the canister.

Secret View

This exposed view shows the position after the silk is inside the gimmick. At this stage, allow the elastic to pull the canister through your fingers and back into your jacket. Keep your hand in a position which still looks as though it holds the silk. Your spectator's view remains as in step 6.

7.

Secret View

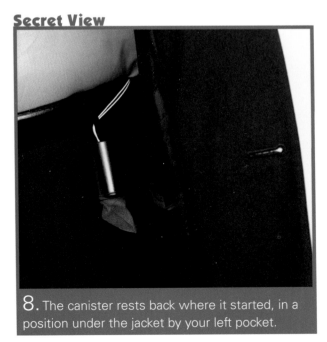

8. The canister rests back where it started, in a position under the jacket by your left pocket.

9. Move both hands to a position in front of your chest and slowly show that they are completely empty. The silk has vanished!

milk to silk

Milk is poured from a jug into a large cup. The cup is turned upside down, but the milk mysteriously fails to fall out! The magician reaches into the upturned cup to reveal that the milk has changed into a white silk handkerchief. This trick creates a beautiful effect and is ideal for larger audiences. For added effect, cut white paper into confetti-size pieces and place them in the folds of the silk before placing the handkerchief in the cup. While performing this effect, it is important that you are aware at all times of the position of the cup in relation to your audience. If you hold the cup too low, the secret will be revealed. A cocktail shaker is the ideal size cup to use.

1. To prepare, carefully measure and cut a piece of cardboard that will divide a cup internally in two. The height of the partition should be about three-quarters the height of the cup.

2. Mold some reusable adhesive around the bottom and side edges of the partition.

3. Push the partition into the cup and secure it to the sides with the adhesive. The idea is to create a watertight compartment.
If you perform this trick on a regular basis, make the partition longer-lasting by using a sheet of plastic and a silicone sealant.

4. Insert a piece of sponge into one side of the cup. You may need to cut the sponge to shape and experiment to determine how much to use. The best sponge to use is the "super-absorbent" type that holds many times its own weight in liquid.

5. To complete the preparation, push a white silk handkerchief into the other compartment. One corner should be near the top, but make sure it is pushed down out of sight.

6. Place the prepared cup on a table, along with a jug full of milk.

7. Begin your performance by carefully pouring some milk into the sponge side of the cup. Once again, experimentation will determine exactly how much milk to use. The milk is absorbed by the sponge.

8. It is wise to wait for a few seconds to ensure that the sponge soaks up all of the milk. Place one hand over the mouth of the cup and get ready to turn it upside down.

9. The slickest way to turn the cup is to allow it to swivel between your left fingers and thumb. When it is upside down, freeze for a few seconds as if something might have gone wrong. This creates a moment of tension and humor if acted well.

10. Take your hand away from under the mouth of the cup and show that the milk has mysteriously defied gravity. Sometimes a small piece of silk will begin to fall from the cup, but this helps to create the illusion that the milk is turning into silk.

11. Slowly pull the silk out completely, allowing it to cascade from the cup.

the trick that fooled houdini

A borrowed watch is placed under a handkerchief and several spectators confirm its presence. In an instant the watch disappears without a trace. Just as mysteriously, the watch can be made to reappear. Rumor has it that one of the world's most famous magicians, Harry Houdini, was fooled by this trick back in the 1920s!

This is one of the few tricks you will learn that requires an assistant, or "stooge." Choose someone who can act well and whom you can trust to keep the secret.

1. Borrow a watch from a spectator. Place it under the center of a handkerchief. Ask several people to reach underneath to verify that the watch is indeed still there.

Secret View

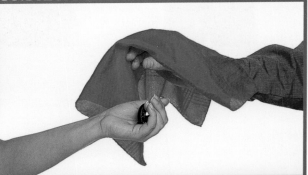

2. The last person to reach under the handkerchief is your stooge, who secretly takes away the watch. To add a simple piece of "misdirection," move the handkerchief away from your assistant's hand as the secret steal takes place. All eyes will follow the handkerchief.

3. Make a magical gesture and whip the handkerchief away to show that the watch has well and truly gone!

thimble magic

A thimble is compact enough to be carried wherever you go and will generate interest as soon as it is made to appear. By linking several of the effects together, a nice routine can be developed. For instance, you could start your routine with the Jumping Thimble, finishing with the Vanishing Thimble and finish with the Thimble Thumb Clip.

jumping thimble

A thimble magically jumps back and forth between two fingers. Although this is a simple stunt, it is amazing how well the illusion works. The trick can also be performed with a finger ring, and is a good impromptu stunt to remember.

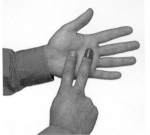   

1. Place a thimble on the tip of the right second finger. Hold the first and second fingers against the palm of your left hand.

2. Tap your fingers against your palm three times. After the second tap, the fingers come approximately 4in (10cm) away from the palm.

3. The first finger quickly curls in and the third finger uncurls.

4. As the fingers reach the palm of the hand, it seems the thimble has jumped. The thimble can be made to jump back by reversing the procedure.

thimble thumb clip

A thimble is caused to disappear and then reappear from the tip of the fingers. Anything that fits on the end of your first finger will work perfectly well. For a really impromptu performance, try using a candy wrapper fashioned into a thimble or a hoop-shaped potato chip. The Thimble Thumb Clip is one of the main sleights necessary to master in order to perform many thimble tricks.

Secret View

 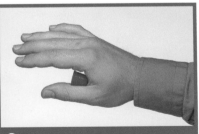 

1. Place a thimble on the tip of your right first finger. Curl your first finger inward so that the thimble rests in the crotch of your thumb.

2. Squeeze your thumb against the thimble and uncurl your finger, leaving the thimble clipped between the base of your thumb and first finger.

3. From the front, the thimble is hidden from view and the hand looks perfectly empty. In performance you will need to be aware of angle restrictions.

vanishing thimble

Once you have learned the Thimble Thumb Clip, you can try the following routine. When executed correctly, the illusion is superb. When you have mastered the trick of making the thimble reappear from behind your hand, you can easily use the same sleight to make it reappear from anywhere you choose, for example from behind the ear of a child or from inside someone else's pocket.

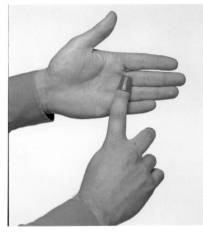

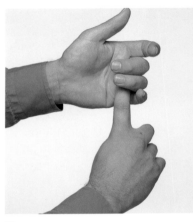

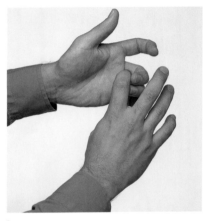

1. Place a thimble on your right first finger, and hold it against the base of the left fingers. Your left palm should face the audience.

2. Curl in your left second, third and fourth fingers. Open the fingers again to show that the thimble is still there, then start to close the fingers as before.

3. Just as the fingers cover the thimble, begin to remove the right first finger, simultaneously raising the hand and placing the thimble into a Thumb Clip.

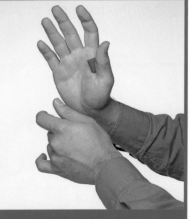

Secret View

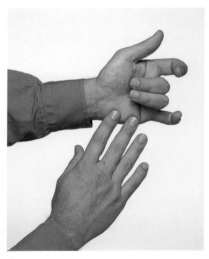

4. This view shows the right hand as it moves upward.

5. The view from the back shows the thimble in the Thumb Clip.

6. Bring the right hand back down to the position shown.

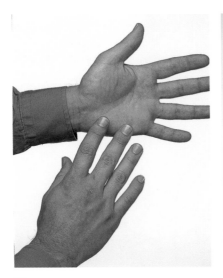

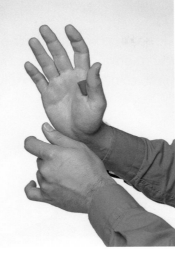

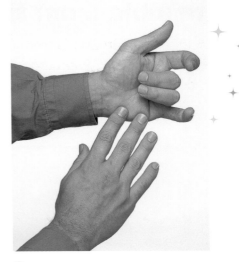

7. Open the left fingers to show that the thimble has vanished. These actions should happen smoothly and briskly. The spectators should not be aware that the thimble has gone from the left fingers until they are opened.

8. Turn the left hand over to show the back of the hand, then show the palm once again.

9. The right hand reaches behind the left and secretly replaces the thumb-clipped thimble on the first finger.

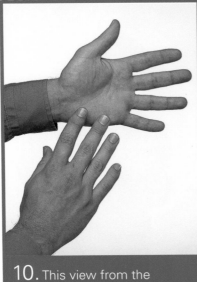

Secret View

10. This view from the back shows the thimble being recovered.

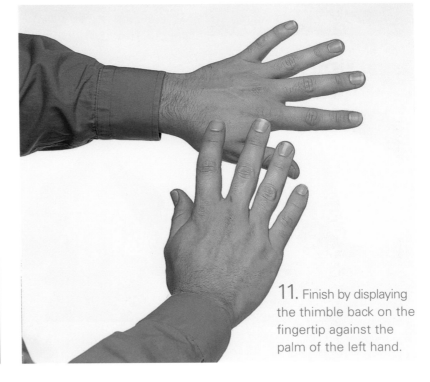

11. Finish by displaying the thimble back on the fingertip against the palm of the left hand.

thimble from silk

A thimble is produced from a silk, ready to be used for other amazing tricks such as Thimble Through Silk. Even though you might not think this is a startling piece of magic, it is a nice visual way to introduce a thimble; better than simply pulling a thimble out of a pocket.

Secret View

1. Hold a thimble in the right-hand Thumb Clip position. Display a silk handkerchief, stretching it between the two top corners with both hands.

2. From the front, all the fingers and the entire silk can be seen, and the thimble remains completely hidden.

3. Cross your arms to show the back of the silk, then uncross your arms again.

Secret View

4. Hold the silk by a corner in the left hand. Your right hand reaches under the silk and retrieves the thimble from the Thumb Clip.

5. Drape the silk momentarily over your right first finger.

6. Whip away the silk to display a thimble on your fingertip.

thimble through silk

A thimble is placed under a silk and visibly melts through the fabric. This trick is the perfect follow-up to Thimble from Silk. Although it is not easy to learn or perform, it is beautiful to watch when performed well. Use a thimble that contrasts with the color of the silk.

Secret View

1. Hold a silk handkerchief with your left hand. It should be clipped between the first and second fingers, draping down the inside of the hand. The right hand displays a thimble on the first fingertip.

2. Hold the silk about chest level and start to move the thimble under the silk. As it passes the left hand, the thimble is secretly placed into the left-hand Thumb Clip position.

Secret View

3. Without hesitation, continue to move the finger under the silk to a position in the center. Under cover of the silk, extend your second finger and bend your first finger backward. This can be seen here through the silk for ease of explanation.

4. Make a gesture with your left hand, which positions itself directly behind the right hand.

Secret View

Secret View

5. During this gesture, push the thimble from the Thumb Clip on to the first finger through the silk. In this view, the silk is lifted for ease of explanation.

6. The first finger straightens behind the second finger. Care must be taken to keep the thimble hidden.

7. From the front, the thimble remains totally unseen.

8. With a shake of the hand, lower the second finger so that the thimble pops into view.

paper magic

A most versatile material, paper is easily available and comes in a wide variety of shapes, colors, sizes, and thicknesses. Of the many tricks that use paper, a few are given here that are simple to prepare and very enjoyable to watch. Cut and Restored Newspaper, together with Snowstorm in China, are perfect for a platform or stage show because they can be seen from a distance.

telekinetic paper

A small piece of paper is folded and stood upright on a table. Apparently using nothing but the power of the human mind, the paper is made to fall over. Is this a true demonstration of telekinesis? No, but it certainly looks like it!

1. For this trick, you will need a small piece of paper, approximately 2¼ x 1¼in (6 x 3cm). The exact size is unimportant but the success of this trick depends on the height of the paper being sufficiently more than the width. Fold the paper in half along its length.

2. Open up the fold to form a "V" shape and position the paper about arm's length in front of you. Due to the height of the paper, it is relatively easy to secretly offset its balance and make it fall over. Rub your first and second finger on your arm, explaining that you are harnessing some static electricity.

3. Gently swing your arm to a position directly in front of the paper but about 6in (15cm) away. As your arm swings around, the air will move and cause the paper to become unstable. As you are a little distance away, the change in air current will take one or two seconds to reach the paper—this will also help to disguise the method to this trick.

4. The paper will fall to the table. Try experimenting with the distance you place between your fingers and the paper. The farther away you are, the better the illusion looks. Despite the fact that the method is very simple, the trick itself is extremely baffling—as you will see when you try this out for yourself.

cut and restored newspaper

A strip of newspaper is unmistakably snipped into two pieces, yet is instantly shown to be restored. This is an ideal trick for a larger audience. It can be performed for a group of children or adults with equal success.

To add to the presentation, invite a member of the audience up on to the stage with you. Give them a pair of scissors and a normal strip of newspaper and ask them to follow your actions carefully. You will always succeed and they will always fail. This can be very comical.

If you plan your moves carefully, after a few demonstrations you could switch your strip with theirs and have the spectator "unexpectedly" succeed. This would be a great finish to the routine.

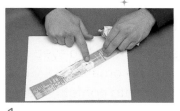

1. To prepare, cut a strip of newspaper from the financial section. The content of such a page will help to camouflage the join. Place the newspaper on top of a scrap of paper to protect the table. Apply a thin layer of rubber cement glue to the middle section of the strip, as shown here.

3. The final piece of preparation is to fold the strip in half with a sharp crease.

2. Wait for the glue to dry completely, then apply some talcum powder to the covered area. This will stop the glued surface of the strip from prematurely sticking at the wrong moment. Blow any excess powder off the newspaper so that everything looks normal.

4. To begin the performance, display the strip of newspaper in one hand and the scissors in the other.

5. Fold the strip in half along the crease and clearly snip off about ½in (1cm) from the center. Try to make the cut as straight as possible. Because of the rubber cement glue, the two separate pieces will be glued back together at the join.

6. Open the strip and the paper will have magically restored itself. You can stop here or repeat the cutting and restoring process. It all depends how much of the strip you covered in glue.

7. Instead of cutting the paper straight, experiment by cutting it at a right angle. You can also place the glue at strategically placed points on the strip of newspaper so that you can begin by actually cutting the strip into two pieces. Then place the two pieces together, cutting again to rejoin them.

snowstorm in china

Several sheets of tissue paper are displayed and torn into strips. They are soaked in a glass of water and squeezed dry. An ornamental Chinese fan is used to aid the drying process and the paper begins to turn into confetti, creating a mini snowstorm that fills the air and covers the stage. This is a spectacular closing effect for a show.

There are several versions of this traditional trick. The following method is the invention of a wonderful Hungarian magician, the Great Kovari. We graciously thank him for allowing us to share his method with you. Many top professional magicians feature versions of this trick in their act.

1. To prepare, cut a strip of flexible plastic, approximately ½ x 4in (1 x 10cm). Pierce a small hole in the center with a sharp point.

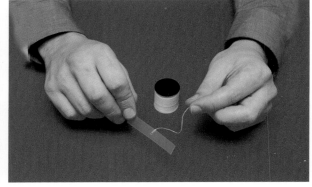

2. Attach a short length of thread to the plastic strip by tying it in a knot through the hole.

3. Use adhesive tape to attach the thread to the back of a fan so that the plastic strip hangs down behind the center.

4. Make a hole in the top of an egg and empty the inside. Wash it out and let it dry completely before continuing.

5. Cut some colored tissue paper into confetti-size pieces. Carefully pack them into the egg.

6. Bend the plastic strip in half, then place it carefully into the hole in the egg so that when the strip expands it grips the sides of the egg securely.

7. Cut two notches into the sides of a box. These will function as a display stand for the fan, as well as a secret holder for the wet tissue.

Secret View

8. Set a table with the fan displayed in the box, a glass of water to the left and some tissue paper sheets at the back of the box. From the back, you can also see the egg hanging from the fan.

9. From the front, there is a pretty display of props and the egg remains hidden behind the fan.

10. To perform, display the various colored sheets of tissue paper and clearly tear them into shreds.

11. Roll up the shreds into a ball and drop it into the glass, soaking the paper thoroughly.

12. Replace the glass on the table and display the wet ball of paper in your right fingertips. Squeeze it dry.

13. Now make a fake transfer into your left hand. Place the ball of paper against the fingers of your open left hand and close it as your right hand comes away with the ball hidden behind the fingers.

Secret View

14. This close-up view shows the position of the hands as they come together. Your body movement should suggest that the ball of paper is really in the left hand.

15. The right hand drops the wad of soggy paper into the box as it reaches for the fan.

Secret View

16. This view from the back shows the paper being dropped as the hand reaches for the bottom of the fan.

17. Hold the fan up with the left hand hidden behind it. Say that you are going to dry the paper by fanning it.

18. With the left hand, secretly pull the egg off the plastic strip. The fan provides a great deal of cover for this.

19. Squeeze the egg tightly, breaking the shell, as you rapidly wave the fan to distribute the confetti pieces as far and wide as possible. The broken eggshell will drop to the floor with the paper, and the evidence will not be noticed. All that is left to do is tidy up!

bending coin (version 1)

A coin is examined and then held in the fingertips. The magician creates an optical illusion that makes the coin look as if it is bending like rubber. This effect can be followed by Version 2, which appears later. To accompany the trick, you could explain that although a coin is made of metal and therefore solid, the magical warmth of your hands can cause it to melt!

1. Hold a coin with both hands, thumbs on the back of the coin, first and second fingers on the front. Allow as much of the coin's surface as possible to be seen by pushing the thumbs forward and pulling the edges of the coin back.

2. This is the view from above, and it can be seen that a good deal of the front surface of the coin is visible.

3. Move both hands inward so that the backs of your hands move toward each other. The thumbs maintain contact with the coin at all times. Move your hands back to the position shown in step 2 and repeat the motion five or six times.

heads I win!

A pocket full of change is emptied on to the table and a small selection of coins chosen. While the magician looks away (or leaves the room) the spectator is instructed to turn over two coins at a time, as many times as desired. Finally they are asked to hide one of the coins under their hand before the magician returns. The magician is able to reveal, with absolute accuracy, whether the hidden coin is heads up or tails up!

1. Throw some change on to a table. You can use any number of coins, but six or seven is perfect. Note whether there are an even or odd number of coins facing heads up. In our example, there are three heads up so we simply remember "Heads are odd."

2. Turn your back and instruct the spectator to turn over two coins at a time, as many times as desired. All the while, keep remembering "Heads are odd." Ask for any one of the coins to be covered before you turn around.

3. Glance at the uncovered coins on the table to see how many coins are now heads up. In our example, there are three. Remember "Heads are odd"? If there are an odd number left, then the hidden coin must be tails up. If there were an even number remaining heads up, then the hidden coin would also be heads up.

4. Assume a hypnotic state, or pretend to receive psychic vibes, then reveal the orientation of the hidden coin. If your instructions have been followed correctly, Heads I Win! will work every single time. Most people carry small change with them, so you can perform this trick at a moment's notice.

explanation
The reason this trick works is because the coins are turned over two at a time, so if there are an odd number of heads facing up at the beginning there will be an odd number of heads facing up at the end, and vice versa.

impossible coin balance

This is a perfect way to win a drink! Challenge your friends to balance a coin on the edge of a banknote. The chances are, no matter how hard they try or how many different ways they attempt to tackle the problem, they will not succeed unless they know the secret.

1. The success of this stunt relies on the use of a crisp banknote. Fold and sharply crease the note in half, along its length.

2. Fold the note in half again, this time along the width. Ensure that the creases are sharp and neat.

3. Place the note on a table so that the folded edge is pointing upward. Position a coin on top of the "V" shape. You may even amaze yourself with the next part!

4. Slowly and gently pull both edges of the note away from each other, straightening the paper. The coin will always find its center of balance and will remain on the folded edge of the note, in an apparently impossible position.

explanation In reality, the short crease is never pulled completely flat and the tiny kink in the paper is enough to stop the coin from falling off. Once the banknote is stretched flat, a steady hand is vital for the success of this trick.

basic coin techniques

Now that you have learned some easy money tricks, it is time to learn a few sleight-of-hand techniques that will enable you to perform some even more amazing magic. Many of these techniques will take time and practice to master, but the outcome is most rewarding.

As suggested earlier in the book, practicing in a mirror will make it much easier for you to correct your own mistakes.

finger palm production

The Finger Palm is an essential grip in coin magic, allowing you to secretly hold and therefore hide a coin (or any small object) in your hand. The coin can then be made to appear from anywhere, using the Finger Palm Production (for example, from behind a child's ear).

Secret View

1. Position the coin at the base of your right second and third fingers. It is held in place by the creases in your skin and by your fingers curling in to hold it. Try to forget that you are holding a coin—look in a mirror to see if you can hold your hand naturally by your side. Your hand should not look as though it were holding anything.

2. You can produce the coin in many different ways. One way is to pretend that you have spotted something floating in the air in front of you. Point it out with the hand is secretly holding the coin.

3. As you reach for the invisible "something," use your thumb to push the coin from its position at the base of your fingers to the fingertips.

4. Try to allow as much of the coin to be seen as possible. The coin seems to appear during the movement between pointing at the floating object and you reaching for it.

5. From the front, it looks just as if you have plucked a coin from thin air.

thumb clip

This is another technique for gripping a coin secretly in your hand. It can also be used to "vanish" a coin. The beauty of this grip is that it allows wide movement of the fingers, while convincingly keeping the coin out of sight.

1. Begin by resting the coin on the right fingers. It should lie flat, in the middle of the first and second fingers.

Secret View

2. Close the fingers into a fist. The coin almost automatically ends in a position that can be clipped by the thumb.

Secret View

3. With the hand open, the coin remains hidden from the front. This exposed view shows the Thumb-Clipped Coin.

classic palm

This is one of the most useful sleights to learn. It enables the performer to hide any small object (in this case a coin) in the palm of the hand, without its presence being detected. The most important aspect of any palm is that the hand must appear natural, so do not hold your hand in an awkward position or move in a way that attracts attention. A common problem is that both the thumb and fourth finger will try to flare out at an unnatural angle, but this will happen less as you learn to relax your hand. After enough practice, your hand will develop tiny muscles that will help you to palm. A palmed object should not be gripped tightly; a gentle touch is all that is required.

1. Place a coin on your outstretched hand. It should lie flat on the tips of the second and third fingers.

2. Keep the fingers parallel to the ground as you turn your hand palm down. The coin should be directly below the palm of your hand.

3. Push the coin into your palm with your second and third fingertips. The exact position of the coin is crucial to success. You may have to move it around a few times and try the coin in slightly different areas of the palm until you feel comfortable.

4. Remove the second and third fingers from the coin, trapping the coin in the palm by gently squeezing the edges between the fleshy pad of the thumb and the area of skin at the opposite edge of the coin.

Secret View

5. This view shows the correct position of the coin. The coin need not be pinched hard. Only a gentle pressure is needed to stop the coin from falling.

6. The coin can be held in the Classic Palm without detection, however it must look natural.

7. In this example, the distortion of the hand is totally unnatural and therefore a clear sign that it hides something.

Secret View

8. Continue your everyday activities (such as writing, typing, and eating) with a coin palmed, and you will soon learn to forget it is there.

downs palm

The Downs Palm is named after the nineteenth-century American magician Thomas Nelson Downs, who is still recognized as one of the finest manipulators of coins ever. This grip is very deceptive as you can show both the front and back of the hand empty before producing a coin. There are angle problems, however, and anyone viewing from too high or too low may glimpse the hidden coin. Practice and check your movements in the mirror—before long you will develop an instinct as to whether or not the coin can be seen. Performed well, this creates a beautiful effect. The coin can be plucked from the air or from any suitable location.

1. Grip the coin between the tips of the right first and second fingers.

2. As the hand closes, the coin should naturally position itself in the crotch of the thumb.

Secret View

3. Open the fingers, leaving the coin gripped in the web between the thumb and the first finger.

4. You can show your hand from both front and back without the coin being seen, as long as you keep the correct angle in relation to the audience.

downs palm production

1. To produce the coin, reverse the above moves. Close your hand, ensuring that the edge of the coin becomes gripped between the tips of the first and second fingers, as seen here.

2. Open your hand, bringing the tip of your thumb on to the edge of the coin and keeping this contact as your hand continues to open.

3. Finally, pinch the coin between your thumb and second finger. Steps 1, 2 and 3 should happen together in one seamless movement.

bobo switch

This is a method of switching one coin for another. It was invented by French magician J.B. Bobo in about 1900, and is still used widely today. The switch is not used as a trick by itself, but being able to switch your coin for a spectator's is an invaluable tool. Bending Coin (Version 2) is an example of the use of the Bobo Switch. Study the following explanation carefully and it will not take too long to learn.

Secret View

1. Hold the coin to be switched in the right-hand Finger Palm position. Borrow a coin from a spectator and hold it clearly displayed in the right fingertips. Hold the left hand out flat.

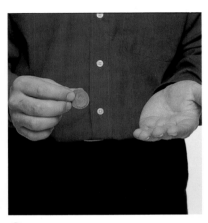

2. From the front, the secret coin is completely hidden in the right palm.

Secret View

3. The switch occurs as the right hand tosses the borrowed coin into the left hand. It goes unnoticed because the coin is in motion the entire time. The right second and third fingers extend to cover the coin and the secret coin is allowed to fall from the Finger Palm position to the outstretched left hand.

Secret View

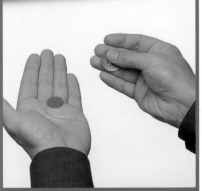

4. Without hesitation, the right thumb pulls the borrowed coin into the Finger Palm position, and the left hand closes around the switched coin.

5. From the front, the action of tossing the coin from one hand to the other looks very natural and should not arouse any suspicion from your audience.

6. Slowly open your left hand to show that the coin has been switched.

coin roll

This flourish is a well-known favorite with audiences worldwide. A coin is rolled across the knuckles in a flourish that looks as magical as it is beautiful. The Coin Roll is a wonderful example of digital dexterity; it is also one of the most difficult things you will learn in this book. You can practice it while you are watching television. Once you have mastered it, try learning it with the other hand and perform two Coin Rolls simultaneously! It is possible to perform the Coin Roll with four coins, each coin rotating ahead of the next.

1. Close your hand into a loose fist. Your knuckles should be parallel with the floor. Begin by balancing a coin on the tip of your thumb.

2. Pinch your thumb against the side of your first finger so that the coin flips on to its edge.

3. Loosen your thumb's grip on the coin so that it balances on the back of the first finger. At the same time, raise your second, third and fourth fingers just enough to clip the coin's edge between the first and second fingers.

4. Raise your first and third fingers while lowering the second finger. This allows you to roll the coin across the back of the second finger.

5. Lower the third finger and raise the second and fourth fingers. The coin will roll across the back of the third finger. Allow the coin to flip over and rest on the side of your fourth finger.

6. Move your thumb under your hand, toward the coin.

7. The coin is transferred to the tip of the thumb, which carries it back under the hand to the start position.

8. You are now in a position to repeat the sequence again.

coin vanishes

There are countless ways to make a coin vanish. The French Drop, Fake Take, and Thumb Clip Vanish are all sleight-of-hand methods and generally should not be used as tricks in their own right. As you become more experienced, you will find that you can incorporate the coin's disappearance into a longer sequence, which can be extra mystifying and a lot of fun.

french drop

This is one of the oldest and best-known techniques used to "vanish" a coin or any other small object. The coin is held in the fingertips of the left hand and supposedly taken by the right hand. In reality, the coin is secretly retained in the left hand. This move should not be shown as a trick on its own, but as a way of "vanishing" a coin within another trick.

1. Display a coin by holding it high in the left finger-tips. As much as possible of the surface of the coin should be seen.

2. The right hand approaches the left to suppos-edly take the coin. The thumb goes under it while the fingers go over it.

3. As soon as the fingers close around the coin and it is out of view, let the coin fall into the left hand.

Secret View

4. The coin falls between the right thumb and the back of the left fingers, almost in Finger Palm position.

5. From the front, it looks as though you pinch the coin with your right fingers and thumb. Watch the coin yourself and actually believe that you are taking the coin.

6. Move the right hand up and to your right, at the same time allowing the left hand (with the coin) to drop naturally to your side. Follow your right hand with your eyes. Your hand should look as though it is actually holding a coin.

tip To make the move more convincing, place a pencil on a table, off to your left-hand side. Hold the coin in the start position. Execute the French Drop, then immediately use your left hand to pick up the pencil. Tap your right hand with the pencil, then show that the coin has vanished. Using the pencil like a wand provides a reason for taking the coin with your right hand—it is more natural to pick up the pencil using your left hand than to reach across your body with your right hand. When executing a sleight, it is very important to justify moves that may look strange if made without a reason.

7. Squeeze your right hand slowly, supposedly shrinking the coin. Open the fingers wide and show the coin is no longer there.

thumb clip vanish

This creates the illusion of placing a coin in your left hand while you secretly retain it in your right hand. It makes use of the technique in magic known as "time misdirection." If you leave enough time between secretly retaining the coin and showing that it has "vanished," the audience will not be able to remember the last time they actually saw the coin or in which hand they saw it. This makes it very difficult for them to reconstruct the method. "Time misdirection" can be applied to many other secret moves and routines.

1. Display a coin on your right fingertips in preparation for the Thumb Clip.

2. Display your open left hand at waist level. Move the left hand up. At the same time begin to close the right hand, placing the coin into the Thumb Clip.

3. Supposedly place the coin on to the fingertips of the left hand, but secretly retain the coin in your right hand.

Secret View

4. The coin falls between the right thumb and the back of the left fingers, almost in Finger Palm position.

Secret View

5. As the right hand moves away from the left and drops to your side, the left fingers close around the "coin." Your eyes must follow your left hand and your body language should suggest that the coin really is in this hand. This exposed view shows the coin in the right hand; in performance it would be hidden in the Thumb Clip or would be allowed to drop into the Finger Palm position.

6. The left hand moves away from your body, to the left. Open the hand and show that the coin has disappeared.

7. To make the move look more natural, give your right hand something to do after it leaves the left hand. Pick up a pencil with the coin in the Thumb Clip. Tap your left hand with the pencil, then show that the coin has gone. Even better, have the pencil in your right pocket and, as you take out the pencil, leave the coin in your pocket.

fake take

Like the French Drop and the Thumb Clip Vanish, the Fake Take enables you to secretly retain an object in one hand while supposedly taking it in the other hand. Try to provide a reason for taking the coin in the right hand—for example, to pick something up with the other hand. This type of sleight should not be used as a trick in its own right, but as part of a longer routine. In some routines the French Drop or Thumb Clip Vanish will be more suitable than the Fake Take. However, it is important to learn several ways to achieve a similar result so that you can choose which looks best. It will not necessarily be the same technique every time.

1. Display a coin on the outstretched fingers of your left hand at about waist height. The coin should be in a position ready for a Finger Palm.

2. The right hand approaches the left hand, supposedly to take the coin. The right fingers lie flat on top of the coin.

Secret View

3. The left hand begins to close as the right hand feigns pinching the coin with the thumb against the fingers. This view from behind shows that in reality the coin remains in exactly the same position, ready to be finger-palmed by the left hand.

4. The right hand swings to the right (with the back toward the audience) as the left hand drops to your left side, supposedly empty, holding the coin in a Finger Palm.

5. As the right hand moves across your body, watch it as you would if the coin was really there. Your body language should suggest that the coin really is in your right hand.

6. Slowly open your right hand to show that the coin has vanished.

sleeving a coin

Magicians are always accused of using their sleeves to secretly hide objects. In fact very few tricks rely on this method, known as "sleeving." There are many different sleeving techniques. If you perfect this method, you will be able to make a coin disappear instantly without the need for any gimmicks. The only requirement is that you wear a jacket with loose-fitting sleeves. The trick will take lots of practice to perfect, and many people give up too soon. If you persevere, you will be rewarded handsomely with a baffling quick trick that will amaze all who see it. Sometimes, even when you know how a trick is done, it still looks magical. Such is the case here.

1. Close your left fingers into a fist. Place a coin on the back of your hand. The coin must be parallel with the ground, otherwise it may fall off.

Secret View

2. Hold your right fingers above the coin. Snap your fingers. As your right second finger snaps off the thumb, it strikes the coin. With practice, if you strike the coin correctly it will automatically sail through the air and up your right sleeve.

3. As soon as the sound of the snap is heard, the coin seems to melt away. Try to keep your left hand perfectly still and as soon as the coin disappears, freeze, so that your spectator doesn't think you tried to sneak the coin away with your right hand.

4. Show both hands back and front. They are unmistakably empty. Keep the right arm slightly bent and be careful not to let the coin fall out of your sleeve.

Secret View

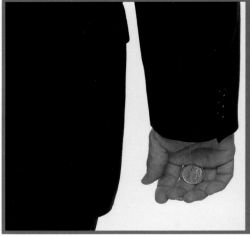

5. You can retrieve the coin by allowing your right arm to hang by your side. The coin will fall from your sleeve and you can catch it in the Finger Palm position.

coin in elbow

You hold a coin in your fingertips and rub it against your elbow. After several apparently unsuccessful attempts the coin seems to dissolve into your elbow, disappearing completely. This is another good example of how "misdirection" works.

1. This is best performed sitting at a table, although you could perform it standing if you alter the handling slightly. Hold a coin in your right fingertips and bend your left arm. (Your left hand should be in a position next to your left ear.) Rub the coin against your elbow. After a few seconds, let the coin fall to the table.

2. Pick up the coin with your left hand and display it on the fingers as you explain that you will try again. Pick up the coin from the left fingers with the right hand. This should be done to look identical to the Fake Take described earlier, which is the move you will be performing later in the trick.

3. Once again repeat the rubbing sequence, only to let the coin fall to the table again. Your audience will become accustomed to these moves, which will help you to accomplish what happens next.

4. Just as before, go to pick up the coin with your left hand and display it in the left fingertips. However, as the right hand approaches to take the coin from the left, execute a Fake Take. Briefly the right fingers mime taking the coin while the left hand returns to a position near the left ear.

Secret View

5. This exposed view shows the coin in the left hand. Secretly slip the coin under the back of your shirt collar to dispose of it. Plenty of "misdirection" is caused by the movement of the right hand, which furiously rubs the supposed coin into the elbow.

Secret View

6. After a few more seconds of rubbing, show that the right hand is empty. The coin has apparently been absorbed into your arm.

7. Display both hands to complete the "vanish." The coin can be recovered later. It will either stay under your collar or fall down your back. Make sure your shirt is tucked in, or the coin may fall out!

handkerchief coin vanish

A coin is placed under a handkerchief and held by a spectator.
The handkerchief is shaken out and the coin seems to melt away.
A specially prepared handkerchief is required. Cut a corner from a duplicate handkerchief.
Stitch it neatly into one of the corners of the handkerchief along three sides. Before stitching the final side, drop a coin into the secret pocket.

1. Show the coin held in the right fingertips. The handkerchief is opened and held by both hands. The special corner is held in the right hand together with the coin. Your right fingers hide the secret pocket.

2. As you move the coin under the handkerchief (aim for the center), take the hidden coin with it. Ask a spectator to hold the coin through the fabric. He will assume he is holding the one shown originally, but it is really the duplicate coin sewn into the corner.

Secret View

3. Allow the loose coin to fall into the Finger Palm position, then remove your hand from the handkerchief in a natural manner.

4. Hold one corner of the handkerchief in each hand and ask the spectator to drop the coin on your command. Count to three and say "Let go!"

5. As he does so, the coin seems to melt away and the handkerchief can be displayed completely empty. You can finish by folding it up and putting it back in your pocket.

clever coin vanish

A coin is placed under a handkerchief and held by a spectator. When the handkerchief is shaken out, the coin melts away. The effect is the same as in Handkerchief Coin Vanish, but the method is very different. This is true of many tricks: there are, for example, dozens of ways of sawing a woman in half! Next time you think you know how a trick is done, take a closer look and see if you really do.

1. To prepare, secretly place a coin into the lining of your tie so that it lies down by the tip.

2. To begin the performance, show another coin in your right hand and an opaque handkerchief in your left.

Secret View

3. Place this coin under the handkerchief, taking the tip of your tie with it. Practice this in front of a mirror.

Secret View

4. Hold the handkerchief at approximately waist height and close to your body so that your tie continues to hang naturally. If you lift your tie too high, your audience will see what you are doing.

5. Ask a spectator to hold the coin, which is really the one in the tie. As in Handkerchief Coin Vanish, allow the other coin to fall into the Finger Palm position, then casually remove your hand.

6. Hold one corner of the handkerchief in each hand and ask the spectator to let go. Display the handkerchief completely empty and hand it to the spectator for examination. He will find nothing.

tip For a complete "vanish," simply hide the coin in the lining of your tie as you place it under the handkerchief. This way you will not have to palm anything. The use of your tie is so subtle that the method will never be guessed by your spectators.

coin wrap

A coin is wrapped in a piece of paper. It can be seen and even felt until the final moment when the paper is torn into pieces and the coin seems to have vanished without a trace. This is an ideal way to "vanish" a marked, borrowed coin, which can then be made to appear in another trick later on in your act (for example, Coin in Egg and Coin in Bread Roll). This is a baffling "any time" coin trick worth learning.

1. You will require an opaque piece of paper approximately 3½in (9cm) square. Place a coin into the center of the paper.

2. Fold the paper upward against the bottom of the coin with a sharp crease.

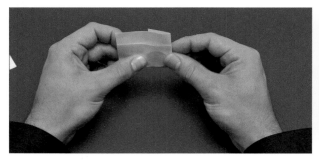

3. Fold the paper to the right and back, behind the coin. Make the creases as sharp as possible.

4. Repeat with the left side of the paper. Be careful not to wrap the coin too tightly, as this will hinder the secret move.

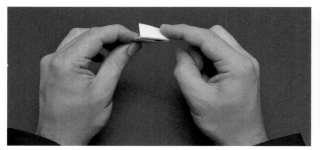

5. Fold the top flap back, at the edge of the paper. It seems as if the coin is trapped, but in reality it can escape from the top of the paper where a gap has been left.

6. Press the coin against the paper with your thumbs, turning the package end over end as you do so. This will position the opening of the packet toward the bottom, while creating an impression of the coin on the paper, proving its presence.

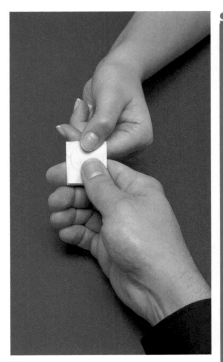

Secret View

Secret View

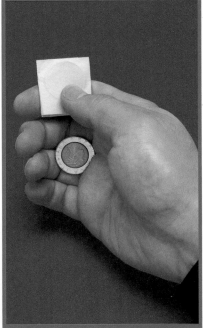

7. Have a spectator verify that the coin is still there. Carefully note the position of the paper at this point.

8. Release your thumb's grip, allowing the coin to fall from the paper. The back of your right hand provides a good deal of cover.

9. The coin lands in the right-hand Finger Palm position. It should fall easily from the paper. If not, your folds at steps 3 and 4 may have been too tight.

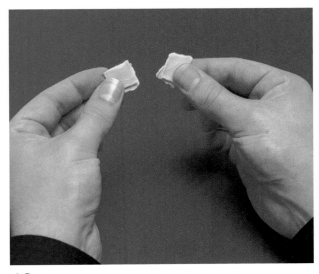

10. Tear the paper in half, then into quarters. The coin remains hidden in the Finger Palm.

11. Toss the pieces of paper on to the table to complete the "vanish." Make the coin reappear in a place of your choice (see More Money Tricks for ideas).

pencil and coin vanish

A coin is held in the fingertips and tapped three times with a pencil. Unexpectedly, the pencil disappears and is found behind the magician's ear! The coin is tapped again and vanishes completely. This routine can be performed at any time, anywhere. Instead of a coin, you can use anything small enough to hide in your hand. This routine is a practical example of how "misdirection" works. It is also a "sucker" trick in that your audience thinks they are let into the secret when in reality you still manage to amaze them.

1. Hold a coin on the outstretched palm of your left hand. Hold a pencil in your right hand. Stand with the left side of your body toward the audience.

2. Tell everyone to watch carefully. Tap the coin three times, each time bringing the pencil up toward your right ear.

Secret View

3. On the third tap, without any hesitation, leave the pencil behind your ear. The first two taps are made to build the expectation that the coin is going to vanish.

4. As your hand descends to tap the coin, open it wide and look amazed as you seem to realize at the same time as your audience that the pencil is no longer there.

5. Explain that you should never reveal the secret to a magic trick, but that you are going to break that rule. Turn your body so that your right side is now toward your audience. Point out the pencil behind your ear.

Secret View

6. As you do this, secretly place the coin into your left pants pocket.

7. Explain that you will do the trick again. Return to the position you were in before, with your left side to the audience. Your left hand should be closed as if it holds the coin. Tap your hand three times with the pencil, then open it to show that this time the coin really has gone.

tip The success of this trick relies on the spectators convincing themselves that the coin is going to vanish. They will be so focused on watching the coin that they will fail to watch the pencil!

more money tricks

This section explains the methods to various tricks that require some of the knowledge learned so far. Coin in Egg uses the Coin Wrap vanish and Bending Coin (Version 2) utilizes the Bobo Switch, while several use palming techniques.

switcheroo

In this trick you introduce a game of hand-eye coordination. A coin is held on the out-stretched palm of a spectator. You explain that you are going to try to grab it before the spectator can close her hand. You manage to grab the coin twice, but fail on the third attempt. When the spectator opens her hand, she see you have not only removed the coin, but will have replaced it with a different coin!

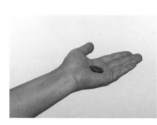

1. For this trick, you will need two different coins. Place one coin on the palm of a spectator's hand.

Secret View

2. Hold the second coin classic-palmed in your right hand. Details regarding the Classic Palm can be found in Basic Coin Techniques.

3. Explain that you will try to grab the coin before the spectator closes her hand, and that she is not allowed to move until you do. Your fingers should be curled in except for your thumb and first finger, which will act like a pair of pincers.

Secret View

4. As the right hand descends, open it fully so that the hidden coin is brought down on to the spectator's finger-tips. The force of this motion will bounce the coin in their palm up in the air.

5. Grab the coin as it bounces, and the spectator will close her hand around the second coin. This occurs so fast it that is impossible for her to feel or see what has happened.

6. The spectator will think you failed, but when she opens her hand, she will see that you have switched the coin!

tip This is a genuine act of sleight of hand, which relies on fast movement and precision timing. With practice you will be able to perform it successfully nearly every time, but it doesn't matter if it takes more than one attempt, because it is not a trick but an example of your dexterity. In order to build a little routine, begin by simply taking the spectator's coin, without performing the switch. It is not as difficult as you might think. Explain that you want to try again and repeat it. The third time, execute the switch.

coin through table

This quick trick will catch people off guard. A coin is made to pass straight through the center of a table. Once you understand the workings of the trick, try using three or four coins and making each coin pass through the table using a different method.

1. With your left hand, tap a coin on the surface of a table at random points, explaining that every table has a particular "soft spot." Display the coin in your left hand in readiness for a Fake Take.

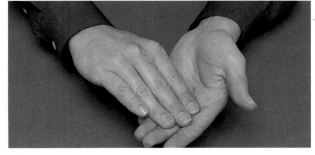

2. Now execute the Fake Take. With your right hand, pretend to pick up the coin. In reality the coin never moves from the left hand.

3. The right hand moves away, pretending to hold the coin in the fingertips. At the same time, the left hand drops below the table to a position directly under the right hand.

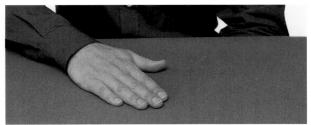

4. Slap the right hand flat on the table, and just at the same moment slap the coin on the underside of the table with your left hand. The result will be a sound that will make the spectators believe that the coin is under your right hand.

5. Pause for a few seconds and then slowly lift your right hand to show that the coin is no longer there.

6. Bring the coin out from below the table on the outstretched palm of your left hand.

coin through handkerchief

A coin is placed under the center of a silk handkerchief. A layer of silk is lifted to confirm to the audience that the coin really is underneath. Very slowly the coin begins to melt visibly through the fabric. The silk is unfolded to show the absence of any holes.

Secret View

1. Hold a silk handkerchief by its edge in the left hand and display a coin in the fingertips of the right hand.

2. Drape the silk over the coin, positioning it directly in the center, as shown here.

3. With the aid of your left hand, obtain a pinch of cloth between the back of the coin and your right thumb.

4. Lift the silk with your left hand to display the coin still held by the fingertips. Note how it is lifted back directly over the arm and above the other half of the silk.

5. Let go with your left hand and flick your wrist down so that both layers of the silk fall forward over the coin. The coin is now outside the silk, hidden under the pinch held by your thumb.

6. Wrap and twist the silk so that the shape of the coin is clearly visible through the fabric. Be careful not to expose the coin accidentally.

7. In this view from behind, you can see that the coin is being held by the fingers and the fabric that surrounds it. Begin to pull the coin up and into view.

Secret View

8. From the front, the coin appears to be slowly melting through the silk. With practice, you will be able to make the coin look as if it penetrates on its own by simply pinching your left fingers together and using your right hand to support the coin as it emerges.

9. Remove the coin completely. Display both the coin and the silk—you can safely hand them to the audience for examination.

coin in egg

This is one of the many methods that exist for producing a coin from nowhere. These can either be used independently, perhaps to introduce a coin that you will proceed to use in another trick, or can follow on from a "disappearing" trick, to make a coin reappear. In this trick, the mystery is increased by vanishing a marked coin borrowed from a spectator. The marked coin is then found inside an egg chosen at random by the spectator. With a little thought, there are many other places that you can make the coin appear from.

1. Borrow a coin from a spectator and ask for it to be marked with a permanent marker pen for later identification.

2. Vanish the coin using any of the methods described earlier. The coin should end up in Finger Palm position. The Coin Wrap would work well here.

3. Display a box of eggs and ask someone to point to any one at random. Lift and display the egg with your left hand.

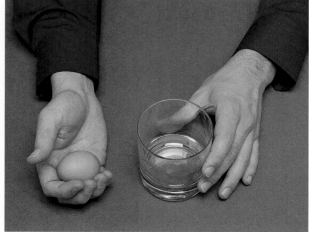

4. Transfer the egg to the right hand, placing it directly on top of the finger-palmed coin. The coin should remain completely hidden from view.

5. The left hand brings a glass to the center of the table, and the right hand taps the egg on the side of the glass, breaking the shell. The eggshell is opened with one hand so that the contents of the egg fall into the glass. Simultaneously allow the finger-palmed coin to drop into the glass with the egg. If timed correctly, it looks just as if the coin falls from the center of the egg.

6. Scoop the coin from the glass with a spoon and have the mark verified as that which the spectator made a few minutes before. Have a napkin ready to wipe the coin dry. Using a similar method, you could also make the coin appear inside other impossible places, such an unopened can of food held by a spectator throughout the trick. The possibilities are endless.

coin in bread roll

In this trick, after "vanishing" a coin, you find it seconds later inside a bread roll that has been sitting on the table the entire time! To make this effect more astonishing, ask someone to mark the coin with a pen so that when they see it again they can be sure that it is the same coin. You could also ask them to choose from a selection of rolls, adding an extra dimension of mystery to the presentation.

Secret View

1. Make a coin disappear, using one of the methods described earlier. Finish with the coin secretly hidden in your right hand. Ask someone to pass you a bread roll. Hold it with both hands so that the coin is hidden on the bottom. This view shows the right hand a split second before the roll is placed on top of the coin.

2. Bend both sides of the roll up so that the bottom splits open. With your fingers, begin to push the coin into the split. This exposed view shows the coin entering the roll. In performance, the bottom of the roll must be pointing down toward the table to hide these actions.

3. Bend the roll in the opposite direction with both hands so that the top cracks open. As it does so, the split at the bottom closes up and the coin appears to come from the center! Ask the spectator to remove the marked coin and verify that it was the one he marked a few moments earlier.

coin through pocket

A coin is held against the outside of the pants pocket and caused to pass through the fabric into the pocket! This quick routine makes use of the Finger Palm. It is quite easy to perfect and makes a good impromptu trick to remember for those times when you are stuck without props. Try to enhance the illusion by using the biggest, shiniest coin you can find.

1. Display a coin held against your right thigh, in line with the bottom of your pocket.

2. With both hands, pinch the fabric underneath the coin. Turn over the coin, simultaneously covering it from view with the fabric.

Secret View

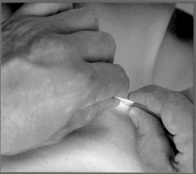

3. Secretly slip the coin into the right-hand Finger Palm position, using your thumb. This is unseen from the front. The photograph here shows your view.

4. With the coin still hidden in the Finger Palm, hold on to the top of the fold with your right first finger. Position your left first finger and thumb under the right and pinch a small piece of fabric.

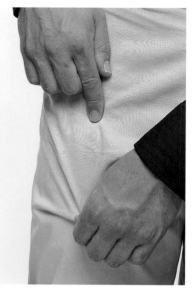

5. Pull the fabric flat and show that the coin has vanished.

6. Reach into your right pants pocket. Remove your hand with the coin displayed clearly at its fingertips.

bending coin (version 2)

Earlier in the book, Bending Coin (Version 1) showed how to create the illusion of a coin bending. You will now have learned the necessary skill to perform a similar type of illusion, which is the perfect follow-up. The amazing thing about this trick is that at the end you give the lender their coin back in its bent condition—a souvenir they can keep forever!

Secret View

1. To prepare, you need to bend a coin. First cover it with a cloth so that you do not mark it. Use a pair of pliers to hold the coin, then bend it with another pair of pliers. The result will be a coin that looks like the one shown here.

2. Before you begin, hide the bent coin in the right-hand Finger Palm position. Begin the performance by borrowing a coin that matches yours, and hold it in your fingertips as shown. Perform Bending Coin (Version 1) as described earlier.

3. At the end, hold your left hand out flat with the coin held in the right fingertips. You now apparently toss the coin from your right hand into the left. In reality, you perform the Bobo Switch, as described earlier.

Secret View

4. This exposed view shows the bent coin lying on your left hand and the right coin about to be placed in the Finger Palm position. There should be no hesitation in your actions.

5. As the coin touches the left hand, it closes immediately into a fist so that the bend remains hidden. Squeeze the coin hard as if you are squashing it.

6. Open your left fingers wide to show that the coin really does have a bend in it. Give it back to the spectator, who will treasure the curiosity and think about it long after the event. As mentioned earlier, Bending Coin (Version 1) is a great prelude to this trick, and together they make a nice, memorable routine.

appearing money

Imagine reaching up into the air and producing real money. You would never have to work again! Your audience doesn't have to know the money was yours to start with. This is one of the best impromptu tricks you can perform. If you set up the trick prior to receiving your bill or check at the end of a meal, you can magically produce a tip for your waiter.

1. To perform this trick, you will need to wear a long-sleeved shirt. Take a banknote and fold it in half, widthways, down the middle.

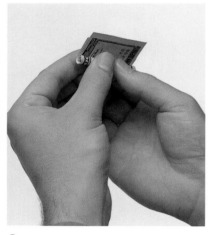

2. Carefully roll the note tightly into a cigarette shape, starting at the fold, as shown here.

Secret View

3. Place the rolled-up note into the crook of your left elbow. Fold over the fabric to hide the note and to keep it in place. Keep your arm bent to prevent the note from falling out.

4. Show your right hand empty, simultaneously pulling your sleeve up with your left hand. This should look very natural, and will make your audience less suspicious when you repeat it.

5. Repeat the motion with your left hand. However, as the right hand tugs the sleeve, it secretly grasps the rolled-up note from the crook of your elbow.

Secret View

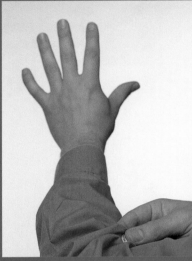

6. The exposed view shows how the left hand creates enough misdirection for this to happen. The right hand secretly retrieves the note, while the audience is focused on making sure that your left hand is empty.

Secret View

7. Bring both hands to a position in front of you, at about chest level. The rolled-up note is held hidden in the right hand. The top end is pinched between the thumb, first and second fingers. These fingers pull the rest of the note back and out of sight.

8. From the front, both hands still look completely empty. This is a very convincing illusion.

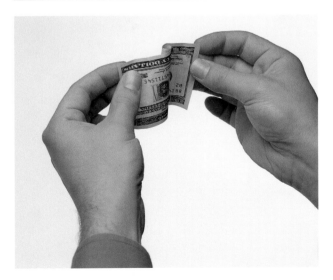

9. Bring your fingers together and, without pausing, use your right thumb to pivot the note into a position which allows both hands to grip an edge each.

10. Snap open the note.

Glossary

banknote A bill of paper money.

camouflage A technique that allows objects or people to remain unnoticed.

canister A cylindrical container.

conjuring The performance of tricks that are seemingly magical, typically involving sleight of hand.

dexterity Skill in performing tasks using the hands.

elastic Stretchable fabric, usually containing a type of rubber.

flourish A bold or extravagant gesture or action, often done to attract the attention of others.

gesture The term used to describe any body action done by a magician during a trick.

illusion A distortion of the senses that leads one to see an action that cannot possibly be occurring.

impromptu Performed with little or no preparation.

lapel The folded flaps of cloth on the front of a jacket or coat.

misdirection A form of deception in which the attention of an audience is focused on one thing in order to distract its attention from another.

ornamental Used for a decorative purpose.

palm Making an object "vanish" through deception.

partition Something used as a divider.

production The act of producing an object out of thin air.

pull An elastic cord used in a magic trick that helps a magician make something appear or disappear quickly.

restriction A regulation that limits access to something.

silicone A rubber-like compound that is typically heat-resistant.

silk A handkerchief used in magic.

sleight A conjuring trick.

stunt An unusual and difficult physical feat or an act requiring a special skill.

telekinetic The ability to create motion in objects without contact or other physical means.

versatile Changing readily.

American Museum of Magic
107 East Michigan Avenue
Marshall, MI 49068
(269) 781-7570
Web site: http://www.americanmuseumofmagic.org
The American Museum of Magic celebrates magicians and their magic. It holds the stories
    and the treasures of performers that entertained residents of the smallest communi-
    ties and audiences in the grandest theaters.

College of Magic
P.O. Box 2479
Clareinch
7740
Cape Town, South Africa
Web site: http://www.collegeofmagic.com
E-mail: fo@collegeofmagic.com
The College of Magic is the only specialist training organization that offers a diploma pro-
    gram in the magical arts for adults and school students alike.

International Magicians Society
581 Ellison Avenue
Westbury, NY 11590
(516) 333-2377
Web site: http://www.magicims.com
This is the world's largest magic society as recorded in the *Guinness Book of World
    Records,* with over 37,000 members worldwide.

The Magic Circle
12 Stephenson Way
Euston
London, UK NW1 2HD
Web site: http://www.themagiccircle.co.uk
The Magic Circle museum is a treasure trove of items from the golden age of music halls.

Society of American Magicians
P.O. Box 505
Parker, CO 80134
(303) 362-0575
Web site: http://www.magicsam.com
The Society of American Magicians, founded on May 10, 1902, in Martinka's famous magic shop in New York City, is the oldest and most prestigious magical society in the world.

Web Sites

Due to the changing nature of Internet links, Rosen Publishing has developed an online list of Web sites related to the subject of this book. This site is updated regularly. Please use this link to access the list:

http://www.rosenlinks.com/MAG/Alaka

Barnhart, Norm. *Amazing Magic Tricks*. Mankato, MN: Capstone, 2008.

Christopher, Milbourne, and Maurine Christopher. *The Illustrated History of Magic*. Philadelphia, PA: Running Press, 2005.

Diaconis, Persi, and Ron Graham. *Magical Mathematics: The Mathematical Ideas That Animate Great Magic Tricks*. Princeton, NJ: Princeton University Press, 2011.

The Diagram Group. *The Little Giant Encyclopedia: Card and Magic Tricks*. New York, NY: Sterling, 2008.

Einhorn, Nicholas. *A Deck of 101 Magic Tricks: Step-by-Step Illusions on 52 Cards*. Leicester, UK: Anness, 2008.

Fajuri, Gabe. *Mysterio's Encyclopedia of Magic and Conjuring*. Philadelphia, PA: Quirk Books, 2010.

Fulves, Karl. *Self-Working Paper Magic: 81 Foolproof Tricks*. Mineola, NY: Dover, 2011.

Jay, Joshua. *Joshua Jay's Amazing Book of Cards: Tricks, Shuffles, Stunts & Hustles Plus Bets You Can't Lose*. New York, NY: Workman, 2010.

Jay, Joshua. *Magic: The Complete Course*. New York, NY: Workman, 2008.

Jones, Graham M. *Trade of the Tricks: Inside the Magician's Craft*. Berkeley, CA: University of California Press, 2011.

Kalush, William, and Larry Sloman. *The Secret Life of Houdini: The Making of America's First Superhero*. New York, NY: Atria, 2007.

Kaufman, Richard. *Knack Magic Tricks: A Step-by-Step Guide to Illusions, Sleight of Hand, and Amazing Feats*. Gilbert, AZ: Knack, 2010.

Leeming, Joseph. *Easy Magic Tricks*. Mineola, NY: Dover, 2008.

Lemezma, Marc. *Mind Magic: Extraordinary Tricks to Mystify, Baffle, and Entertain*. Middlesex, UK: New Holland, 2005.

Maskelyne, Jasper. *Maskelyne's Book of Magic*. Mineola, NY: Dover, 2009.

Ogden, Tom. *The Complete Idiot's Guide to Street Magic*. Royersford, PA: ALPHA, 2007.

Rapaport, Brooke Kamin. *Houdini: Art and Magic*. New Haven, CT: Yale University Press, 2010.

Steinmeyer, Jim. *The Last Greatest Magician in the World: Howard Thurston Versus Houdini & the Battles of the American Wizards*. New York, NY: Tarcher, 2011.

Stone, Alex. *Fooling Houdini: Magicians, Mentalists, Math Geeks, and the Hidden Powers of the Mind*. New York, NY: HarperCollins, 2012.

Thorley, Julia. *Simple Conjuring Tricks: For Everyone*. Slough, UK: Foulsham, 2005.

Zenon, Paul. *Street Magic: Great Tricks and Close-Up Secrets Revealed*. Philadelphia, PA: Running Press, 2007.

INDEX

About the Author

Nicholas Einhorn is a "Gold Star'" member of The Inner Magic Circle. In 2011 he "fooled" two of the world's most famous magicians on the UK TV show *Penn & Teller: Fool Us.* He subsequently won a trip to perform alongside Penn and Teller in Las Vegas. Nicholas has won a number of industry awards for his work, including: The Magic Circle Centenary Close-up Magician 1905–2005; F.I.S.M (World Magic Championships) Award Winner 2003; The Magic Circle Close-up Magician of the Year 2002; and The Magic Circle Close-up Magician of the Year 1996. Nicholas performs at events and parties throughout the world as well as uses his magic to build crowds for some of the world's largest companies at business trade shows and exhibitions. Nicholas is regularly invited to lecture at magic societies and conventions the world over. As a magic consultant, Nicholas has designed and created the special effects for several large-scale stage productions as well as being a consultant on several feature films. He also develops and markets new magical effects for the magic fraternity. To date, his illusions have been purchased and performed by magicians all over the world, including some of the biggest names in magic, such as Paul Daniels and David Copperfield.